20 Poems Has October...

Claire Williamson

BookLeaf Publishing
India | USA | UK

Presentation by *BookLeaf Publishing*

Web: www.bookleafpub.com

E-mail: info@bookleafpub.com

ISBN: 978-93-5744-992-2

First edition 2022

DEDICATION

To my family and friends. You know who you are.

ACKNOWLEDGEMENT

Thank you to Bookleaf Publishing for this opportunity. A goal reached and a dream realised.

PREFACE

In order to complete this, I remembered The Details:

Recognise YOUR demons,
Light a candle for your PAST SELF,
See what was, what IS, and what can be,
Find a goal you can be PROUD of, and then
Nothing can get in the way OF YOU.

The Change.

Spring
is blossom;
pink and cream
floating on green branches;
delicate as the first fingers
of warmth from the sun.
This, a prelude to the main event
– summer – fresh green leaves, rustling
with breathy breeze, perfect balance of shade
as light flickers through the branches to land
on the ground like spotlights on a stage.
Eventually, winter will be upon us,
with shivering twigs and frost-laden boughs.
It seems a distant memory at the moment; but it
will be here all too soon, and the occasional snap
of ice, or the chill of a raindrop
reaching you through the maze
of rustling fronds,
means that you never quite
forget.
But, right now,
it is the beginning
f autumn, the
biggest
change of
all. Sudden
cold, crackling leaves,
and falling hues of brown
and gold.A yearly change,
and somehow, we are never ready.

Ascertained.

I visit you every day
To make sure you still exist.
Doctors say you're fine
Like this;
You won't die
On life support
(But neither will you live).
But I like to make sure –
To be certain, if you will –
That you're still there,
Existing.
So I visit you every day.

The House.

The house at the end is all lonely and bent,
Like an old man at the end of his days,
To love and to cherish her would be time well
spent,
But right now, she just stands in the way.

The village on the coast is neglected and worn,
Like a forgotten old friend, or a long-broken
vow,
To invest and to prioritise would be to prevent
need to mourn
But right now, that's time people don't allow.

The country is locked in anticipation and worry,
Like the gap between lightning and thunder's
boom,
To speak and to be heard, we'd do well to hurry,
But right now, people have better things to do.

The planet is singing a sad lament,
Like an unloved child, desperate for a say,
To love and to cherish her would be time well
spent,
But right now, she just stands in the way.

Hidden Features.

The Schoolgirl who likes to skateboard,
The Choir who love to dance,
Or the Accountant who buys more than he can afford
(When given half a chance).

The Writer who loves to be read to,
For then he can escape the strain,
Of needing to be one of the original few,
To write words which 'change the game'.

The Comedian who cries at rom-coms,
The Scientist who follows a faith,
Or the Driver who'll fish for hours in his pond
(Despite the change of pace).

A game that has the highest stake;
The Judge who lets down his guard,
When the decision is no longer his to make,
The future on the turn of a card.

The nurse who loves to be cared for,
The Vicar who needs to confide,
The Ventriloquist who's after something much
more

Than a puppet's shadow can provide.

All these Hidden Features are there,
In a world that's made for us to see,
That happiness is found almost anywhere,
If you are just you and I am just me.

Is It So Hard?

I don't believe in the smile that you leave,
When you say goodbye,
Well I don't expect the world to move me,
But for God's sake could you try?

There's no trace of you in us anymore,
Tell me, where is your heart?
Only so much that we can endure,
But to end it, where do we start?

How do you repair that which never was whole,
How do you turn back time?
And even if we did, we would, we could,
Will you ever really be mine?

Is it so hard to continue this love?
Is this so hard to believe?
I wonder if I'm alone in knowing,
That this is worth more to achieve.

Because no, I don't believe in the smile that you
leave,
When you walk out and say goodbye,

And though I don't expect the world to move
me,
I wonder, for God's sake, would you try?

In Retrospect.

If I wrote a letter to myself,
Left it carefully to be found
By myself, in some long distant past
Then I wonder, where would it be bound?

Is there a part I'd like to change?
Or is there a story worth sharing?
An event, a moment, a decision made,
On which my wisdom could have bearing?

What about a time, a lifetime ago,
A wrong decision made about my future,
But youth it seems needs time to grow
And dreams need time as a tutor.

Or maybe, it might've helped when
A relationship went stale or cold,
But the people you keep as time circles again
Are worth more than their weight in gold.

I suppose what they say about hindsight
Is a point well made for them,
But who are they, to decide my decisions made,
When I wasn't the same person back then?

So I'd write a letter to myself,
And tell me not to worry,
'Cause experience is won through decisions
made,
And that's something foresight shouldn't sully.

(In A) Fix.

Might you have such thing
As a piece of string,
To tie my world back together?
It might seem so small
For one once standing so tall,
But I suppose now
Is better late
Than never.

Wishful Thinking.

Oh to the days, when I won't make a mess,
Won't have to think, or second-guess,
'Cause surely when I'm all grown up,
I won't be a know-it-all, but I'll know enough.

I'll know the answers without having to look,
At Google, or Siri, or even a book,
I'll be a little lazy, but that's ok you see,
'Cause by then I'll feel a bit better being me.

Oh to the days, when the questions I'll ask,
Will be How can I help you? or What is the
task?
And not wondering whether there's a way to
know,
My four times tables better than Joe.

As a grown up I'll know just what to do,
To show I can get there, to beat the queue,
I'll have a good job, and look really cool,
And never use anything I learned at school.

When I'm grown up I'll be successful and good,
At all I need to be, I'll be more understood,

So I'll do my best now, and try not to scoff,
And oh to the days, when all this pays off.

A Poem Of Hope.

A little blade of grass had grown,
Between the crumbling cracks of stone.

It wasn't very big at first,
But that didn't detract from its worth,
As it freed itself from the earth.

Slowly, time came and went,
The grass continued its ascent,
Through seasons, chaos and cement,
It yet it still remained unbent.

We mined and built, and found new ways
To put our visions into play.
And gradually the world became more grey
As Nature became our latest prey.
Earth's olive branch, thrown away.

Perhaps it was in fact mistook,
That our inventions can do more good,
But Nature will do things by the book,
And fix the things that we forsook
Because all you have to do is look,
At Nature's Earth, beneath your foot…

And look…

A little blade of grass has grown,
Between the crumbling cracks of stone.

Assumptions.

A conversation
Repeated.

"I remember falling."
"I remember when my friend fell."
"I remember when you told me about your
friend who fell."
"I remember when you told me of the friend of a
friend who fell…"
"I remember what you told me about falling.
How did you know?"
"I remember when you told me about what your
friend said about falling."
"I remember when you told me about your
friend who knew someone who fell."
"I remember when you told me about falling..."

An assumption
Made.

"I remember falling head-over-heels."
"I remember when my friend fell
head-over-heels."
"I remember when you told me about your
friend who fell head-over-heels."

"I remember when you told me of the friend of a
friend who fell head-over-heels…"
"I remember what you told me about falling
head-over-heels. How did you know?"
"I remember when you told me about what your
friend said about falling head-over-heels."
"I remember when you told me about your
friend who knew someone who fell
head-over-heels."
"I remember when you told me about falling
head-over-heels..."

An emotion
Created.

"I remember falling head-over-heels in love."
"I remember when my friend fell
head-over-heels in love."
"I remember when you told me about your
friend who fell head-over-heels in love."
"I remember when you told me of the friend of a
friend who fell head-over-heels in love…"
"I remember what you told me about falling
head-over-heels in love. How did you know?"
"I remember when you told me about what your
friend said about falling head-over-heels in
love."

"I remember when you told me about your
friend who knew someone who fell
head-over-heels in love."
"I remember when you told me about falling
head-over-heels in love..."

Ruminations.

She came and sat beside me,
On the low stone wall,
Sensing I was the one,
To ruminate on it all.

Her peers played away from us,
And she was left alone,
Sensing space was needed,
While her seeds were sown.

"Do you know what it looks like?
This world, still new to me?
Do you remember the time it took
To understand, to see?"

I shake my head no,
For it's true, I do not,
Maybe once I knew,
But it seems I forgot.

She continues without me,
Knowing I'll catch up,
"To me, it looks broken,
Before it's begun.

"We are animals, aren't we?
I learned that at school.
Yet all the other animals
They are never so cruel.

They look after each other,
And they live, as best they can,
But they don't hurt for fun,
They stick to Earth's plan.

Yet we think we're different,
That we're better, deserve more,
How can we say that
When we create the war?

We fight against everything,
The world and our lives,
We even fight each other,
And we try to divide.

We fight against change,
That make us feel unsafe,
Of course, Black Lives Matter,
In theory about race.

But in practice it is harder
To feel we can adapt
When you've known only one way,
How do you react?

Everyone is equal,
Men and women just the same,
But it's harder to imagine,
When you call objection by its name,

And what about other genders,
And who we like and love?
And what we like and eat and drink,
And our beliefs about above?

We're so divided in this world,
We've can't find the way back out,
I have these thoughts it will get worse,
Because we have so much doubt.

It seems too big a problem
We can't solve it one by one,
We need to work together,
Until it's all undone.

I wish it could be easier,
I dream we'll soon be free,
I have ideas I want to try,
So that I can be happy as me.

"Tell me where you live,
I'll send you all my dreams,
The ones where I see it all

And it's worse than it seems.

"But I'll send you others
That aren't so sad
That way you'll see
That it's not all bad."

How simple her sermon,
How clear her words,
And all I can do now,
Is honour their worth.

She came and sat beside me,
On the low stone wall,
Sensing I was the one,
To ruminate on it all.

Forget.

Forget I met you
- For when I did

The world stopped spinning,
With daily life dimming,
Your presence, a rarity,
And it gave me the clarity,
To know that nothing could be better.

Forget I knew you
- but when I have

The world is brighter,
And then I feel lighter,
Achievements unlimited,
And I feel in my element,
It feels like everything is better.

Forget I need you
- 'Cause when I do

The world is too much,
And you become my crutch,
I can't function without you,
Helpless, there's nothing I can do,

And almost anything is better.

Forget I love you
- As when I do

The world stops spinning,
Daily life still dimming,
And it still amazes me
Just how I can be so crazy,
To think that nothing can be better.

I Can't Stay.

It's the hardest thing I'll ever have to do,
To look into your eyes, and tell you I don't love
you.
It's the hardest thing I'll ever have to lie,
To show no emotion, when you start to cry.

Maybe another time, another day,
As much as I want to… I can't stay.

It's the saddest thing I'll ever have to see,
To watch the tears on your face, all caused by
me.
It's the saddest thing I'll ever have to know,
To realise I'm destroying you, as I stand up and
go.

Maybe another time, another day,
As much as I want to… I can't stay.

It's the cruelest thing I'll ever have to cause,
To know I'll make you crumble, as I walk out
those doors.
It's the cruelest thing I'll ever have to say,
To tell you it's over, as I slowly turn away.

Maybe another time, another day,
As much as I want to… I can't stay.

It's the strongest thing I'll ever have to do,
To convince myself it's best, as I say I don't love
you.
It's the strongest thing I'll ever have to hide,
To have said I never loved you, yet inside
knowing I lied.

Maybe another time, another day,
As much as I want to… I can't stay.

The End.

(No)
I'm not doing this, no not anymore,
'Cause you know it's just like you said before,
It seems so safe, so secure, and yet,
We're flying without a safety net,

(Can't)
Why mistake the risk for something worth
giving,
A misguided way to keep this love living,
If it was worth the love, the patience, the time,
Then this doubt would have less reason than
rhyme,

(Please)
I'm not doing this, no not anymore,
'Cause you know it's just like you said before,
It seems so safe, so secure, and yet,
We're flying without a safety net,

(And)
On a knife edge ain't no way to live,
Just scratch the surface and something must
give,
And if we fall, then we lose it all,
Why gamble on the impossible?

(Verb) To Interact.

I repeat myself a lot.

It's a symptom,
A by-product of
Spending so long
With nothing to talk about
But teaching.

No hobbies,
Social interactions,
News, or current affairs.
No inner turmoils,
Favourite tv, music or
Anything much which was relatable
To the experiences of others.

I had nothing
To have a conversation about,
And yet the very lonely nature
Of the teaching profession
Means that I was desperate for
Interaction,
Of value, outside
When I could no longer find it
In the classroom.

So I repeat myself a lot.

And if I'm getting tired
Of hearing the same things
Come out of my mouth
Then how must they feel?
So I learn that it's better to stop myself.

And now I sit
With those I'm close to
And desperately seek
Topics of conversation,
Yet I have nothing of value to offer.

And the interaction I craved
Is becoming something
Stilted and ugly,
And I don't know
How to fill the gap.

The very thing
Driving the pieces of me
Further apart,
It seems,
Was also the glue
Holding them together.

After the cacophony of noise

That was the classroom,
I have blessed silence.

But which is better company?

The irony is this:
Teaching was preventing me
From having those relationships,
Those conversations,
With my friends and family.
And now the lack of teaching
Threatens to do the same thing.

Penance.

So maybe this is it,
What its always meant to be,
Maybe it's what's needed,
But – for God's sake – not to me.

Maybe all that's happened,
Has led me now to this,
Maybe it's a penance,
For some long forgotten bliss.

Maybe it's required,
It's what the fates allow,
Maybe there's no stopping it,
But – for God's sake – not here, not now.

Maybe its deserved,
With no blame but my own,
Maybe the the result of something,
I should have left well alone.

Maybe it's a result,
Of a problem that I've missed,
Maybe I had it coming,
But – for God's sake – not like this.

Maybe if I could change the past,
Then all would now be fine,
Maybe hindsight is just a curse,
For I can't go back in time.

Maybe I invited this,
Retribution to make me see,
That being sorry is no longer enough,
But – for God's sake – let it be.

Staged Release.

The Start:

Make it so
It's hard to let go
And I will be your forever.
But make it seem
That's not what you mean
And we will have lost our tether.

I am with you, and I know,
How to be strong - I feel aglow.
And now I've found, it's the right time,
To take back, all that's mine...

The End:

This is our time over,
I wish I did it sober,
But I pushed my back against the wall.
And though there's no mistaking,
All the time it's taken,
Now it's my time to have it all.

I was so lost, I didn't know,
How to be strong, and let go.

But now I've found, it's the right time,
To take back, all that's mine.

Behind the disguise,
A burden in your eyes,
You did not need to watch me fall.
But now my fears are conquered,
And I'm moving onward,
And what comes now is my call.

I was so lost, I couldn't see,
How to move on, and let it be.
But now I'm ready, I can go on,
All my previous doubts have gone.

So this is our time over,
And though I wish I did it sooner,
Before, I had only the strength to crawl.
And though there's no mistaking,
All the time it's taken,
Now it's my time, and I will stand tall.

Circumstance-19.

I am fortunate.
I am healthy.

No symptoms, no isolation
Minimal testing
(Only what is required)
And no problems following the rules.

I am fortunate.
Potentially vulnerable
- but only minor -
And working from home
Has made things better
And can continue.

I am fortunate.
I have gained experiences
Opportunities
I would have never had in the old normal.
Saved money,
A space of my own
Huge life changes
That make the future brighter.

I am fortunate.

It's all I can think about
When I see the world now
In so many ways
I am lucky
And I feel that I can understand
Empathise
And support others,
But how much can I give
Without the experience of misfortune?

I am fortunate.
But what does that make me?

The Problem With Forever.

The problem with forever is -
It's too good to be true,
Never considered seriously,
Never to happen to you.

The problem with forever is -
It's just another word,
An unfathomable quantity,
Overused, undeserved.

The problem with forever is -
It's just there, out of reach,
A constant goal, an affirmation,
With importance we mis-teach.

The problem with forever is -
It always starts too soon,
Unnoticed, and so uncharted,
Constantly fine tuned.

The problem with forever is -
It never seems enough,

Unworthy of devotion,
Like an ocean deemed too rough.

The problem with forever is -
Something has to give,
Unyielding love no longer adapts,
"Unlove" learns to outlive.

The problem with our forever was -
It came and went too soon,
Love can only do so much
When it can't get past the moon.

Maybe I'll Write A Poem About Making Resolutions.

Maybe this year I'll make a resolution,
Maybe I'll look at it as finding a solution,
Or maybe I'll feel like I'm following the crowd,
As I promise myself something that last year
many vowed.

Maybe I'll choose something that fits the norm,
Maybe to eat less, to exercise, something of that
form,
Yet maybe I'll be looking for the world to see,
That I'm ready to make these changes in me.

Maybe I'll look to the physical to change,
Maybe move house, job or area, now there's
such a range,
Or maybe I'll discover something previously
unknown,
That gives me joy much closer to home.

Maybe I'll promise to be better and good,
Maybe I'll promise to be more understood.
And maybe my promises will go on, or maybe
they'll stay,
They all sound so easy when said this way.

Maybe resolutions will happen, maybe they'll
die,
Maybe I'll console myself knowing that I tried,
And maybe I'll make excuses, or maybe I'll see,
That it's not about the promise: it's about what I
can be.